S0-BDP-193

The MIGHTY BIG BOOK OF Optical Illusions

GALLERY O' GAMES

TO ONE OF THE MOST
CREATIVE PERSONS I HAVE THE
THRILL OF KNOWING. YOU *ALSO*
HAPPEN TO BE MY *DAUGHTER!*
ALL MY *LOVE* TO YOU,
VALISSA!
--DAD.

ISBN 978-0-8431-7791-6   Q R S T

The Mighty Big Book of Optical Illusions

Craig Yoe

WEBMASTER OF
WWW.RIDDLES4KIDS.COM

GALLERY O' GAMES

PSS!
PRICE STERN SLOAN

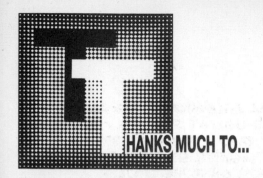

THANKS MUCH TO...

JON ANDERSON AND **KELLI CHIPPONERI,** OUR FAVORITE EDITORS; **JAYNE ANTIPOW,** INDEFATIGABLE VICE PRESIDENT OF PROJECT MANAGMENT EXTRAORDINAIRE; **PATRICIA PASQUALE,** POWERFUL PROSE PRODUCER AND PROOFREEDER (OOPS); **WAYNE TREPTOW,** THE INCREDIBLE DESIGNER WHO COULD; **ROSALIE LENT,** AS ALWAYS; **LUKE MCDONNELL,** THE FASTEST DRAW IN THE WEST; **AMANDA BONAVITA,** THE ILLUSTRIOUS ILLUSIONER; **KENDALL VALENTINE,** THE SUPER SAVER; **SCOTT KIM,** FOR PERMISSION AND INSPIRATION; **ADELE KURTZMAN** AND **DENIS KITCHEN,** AND **DON ORIOLO** FOR THEIR KINDNESS; AND **CLIZIA GUSSONI,** JUST THE BEST DARN DESIGNER THE WORLD WILL EVER KNOW, AND THAT'S NO **ILLUSION!**

OPTICAL ILLUSIONS ARE ALL AROUND US. WE PROBABLY COME ACROSS THEM *EVERY DAY.* WHICH MAKES ME *WONDER...* IS *THIS PAGE* JUST AN *ILLUSION?* IS THIS *REALLY* A BOOK, OR DOES IT JUST *APPEAR* TO BE A BOOK? *OUCH.* NOW MY *HEAD HURTS.* SURE, YOU THINK IT'S PRETTY FUNNY *NOW,* BUT WE'LL SEE HOW *YOU* FEEL AFTER READING THIS BOOK O' *MIND BENDERS* AND *CHICKEN TENDERS* (WELL, WE DIDN'T HAVE *ROOM* FOR THE *CHICKEN TENDERS,* BUT ENJOY THE *MIND BENDERS* ANYWAY)!

YOUR PAL,

CRAIG YOE

YOE!

WARNING:

THE *ILLUSIONS* IN THIS BOOK CAN
BE *PRETTY TRICKY!* DON'T WORRY,
I'VE PROVIDED THE *ANSWERS* FOR *YOU*,
JUST IN CASE YOU GET *STUMPED!*
TO READ THE ANSWERS WRITTEN IN *STRETCH TYPE*
(LIKE THE ONE ON THE *BOTTOM* OF
THE *NEXT PAGE*), DO WHAT THIS *GUY*
IS DOING: HOLD THE BOOK *FLAT* AT
EYE LEVEL, CLOSE ONE *EYE*, AND *READ ON!*
TRY IT WITH THE *PUZZLE* ON THE NEXT *PAGE*...
DID *YOU* GET IT? IT READS, *"THEY'RE NOT – IT'S
THE BACKGROUND PLAYING
TRICKS ON YOU!"*

MIND BENDING!

THOSE *THICK WHITE LINES* LOOK *BENT,* DON'T THEY?

THEY'RE NOT - IT'S THE BACKGROUND PLAYING TRICKS ON YOU!

ADD 'EM UP!

THIS IS ONE *MIXED-UP* ADDITION PROBLEM!

ЗИО
ЗИИ
_____

ИЗТ

CHECK IT RIGHT BY HOLDING IT UP TO A MIRROR!

GOOD LOOKING!

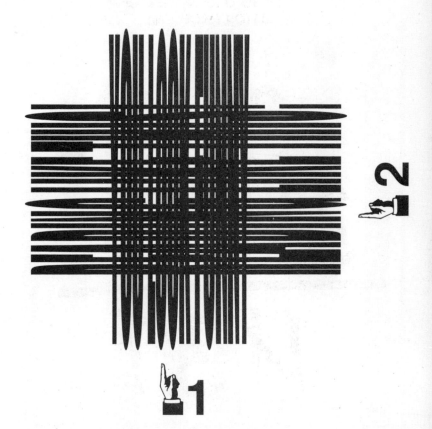

HOLD THE BOOK *HORIZONTALLY* AT
EYE LEVEL. LOOK *ACROSS* THE PAGE IN
THE *DIRECTION INDICATED,* AND READ
THE *HIDDEN MESSAGE!*

NO WAY!

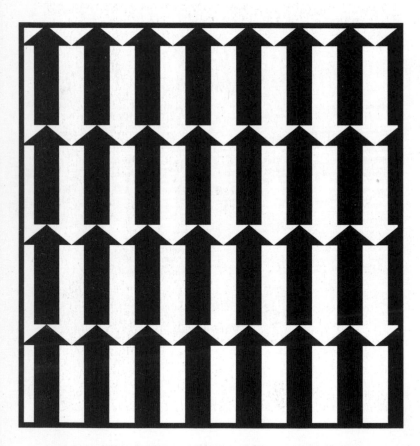

ARE THE ARROWS **WHITE** AND POINTING **DOWN**, OR BLACK AND POINTING **UP?**

IT'S AN ENIGMA!

ABC OR 12 13 14? IS THE *MIDDLE FIGURE* THE LETTER *B* OR THE NUMBER *13?*

SWiTCH-A-ROO #7!

IS THIS A **FEROCIOUS DOG** WITH ITS **MOUTH OPEN** OR IS IT A **CAT** WITH ITS **PAWS** IN **FRONT** OF IT? FLIP THE PAGE **UPSIDE DOWN** AND **DECIDE!**

SEEING SPOTS!

LOOK AT THIS BUNCH OF **LINES.**

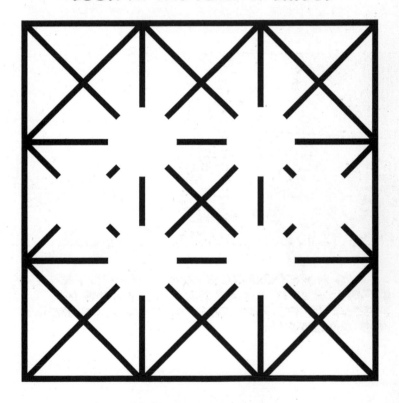

YOU'LL BE SEEING SPOTS WHERE THERE AREN'T ANY!

JUMP FIDO JUMP!

HOLD THIS PAGE IN *FRONT* OF YOUR *FACE,*
AND HOLD YOUR *INDEX FINGER* IN FRONT
OF THE PAGE. *CLOSE ONE EYE,* THEN THE
OTHER – KEEP DOING THAT!

FE-LiNES!

LOOK CLOSELY, THIS ISN'T JUST A **SIMPLE SKETCH** OF A **CAT!**

INCREDIBLE!

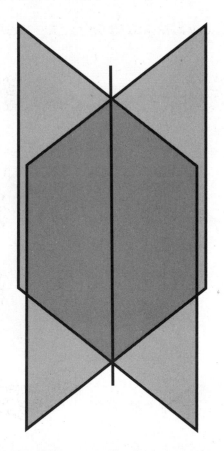

LOOK CLOSELY AT THIS **FIGURE.** WHAT DO YOU **SEE**? THE **TOP** OF IT? TAKE ANOTHER **LOOK.** DO YOU SEE THE **BOTTOM** NOW? **COOL!**

WiLD!

HOW MANY *CIRCLES* ARE THERE?

¡ SPIRAL!

THIS IS ONE OF THOSE *ILLUSIONS* THAT WILL
DRIVE YOUR EYES *CRAZY!* THE LONGER YOU
LOOK AT IT, THE MORE IT *PULSATES!*
SOME PEOPLE EVEN SEE A *LIGHT YELLOW
SHADOW* APPEAR!

LOOK AT THAT!

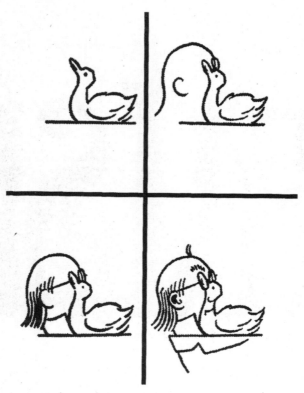

THIS **MAN'S BEARD** IS JUST **DUCKY!**

TRUE OR FALSE?

FALSE / TRUE

© Scott Kim; visit www.scottkim.com

THE ANSWER IS *BOTH!*

EERIE!

STARE AT THE **SKELETON** FOR **30 SECONDS**,
THEN LOOK AT THE **BLACK** AREA.

SUCKER!

IS THIS A *PERFECT* CIRCLE? *YES!*

ROD-iCAL!

THIS **FISHING ROD** SURE IS DECEPTIVE! LOOK AT THE **LINES** OF THE ROD **BELOW** THE SIGN. WHICH ONE DO YOU THINK **CONTINUES** THE LINE **ABOVE** THE SIGN?

YOU'RE STARING!

THIS IS **COOL!** THE **PATTERN** LOOKS LIKE IT'S **MOVING,** ESPECIALLY WHEN YOU **ROCK** THE PAGE **BACK** AND **FORTH!** IT ALSO LOOKS **3-D!**

ALPHA-BOB!

MY FRIEND BOB'S *FACE* IS MADE UP OF *EVERY LETTER* OF THE *ALPHABET!* DON'T *BELIEVE* ME? I *PROVE* IT ON THE *NEXT PAGE!*

BY GEORGE!

DOES THIS **PATTERN** LOOK LIKE **ANYTHING** TO YOU?

SQUINT YOUR **EYES**, IT'S A **PICTURE** OF **GEORGE WASHINGTON!**

OLD FLAMES!

Art by Luke McDonnell

A **CANDLE** OR **TWO PEOPLE** FACING EACH OTHER?

iN THE SHADOWS #1

CREATE YOUR OWN *ILLUSION!* HAVE AN *ADULT* HELP YOU MAKE A *RABBIT* APPEAR BY HOLDING YOUR *HANDS* AS SHOWN IN FRONT OF A *STRONG LIGHT* IN A *DARK ROOM!*

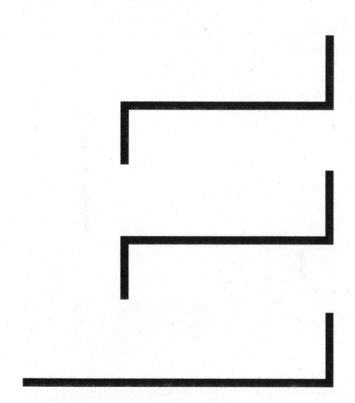

E-KABOO!

IS THIS JUST A SERIES OF **BLACK LINES** OR IS IT A **WHITE LETTER E?**

TAKE A LOOK!

IF YOU READ BETWEEN THESE *LINES,* YOU'LL SEE
THAT EACH *BOX* CONTAINS A *LETTER,* AND THE
LETTERS FORM A *QUESTION.* SEE IT?

CHEW ON THIS!

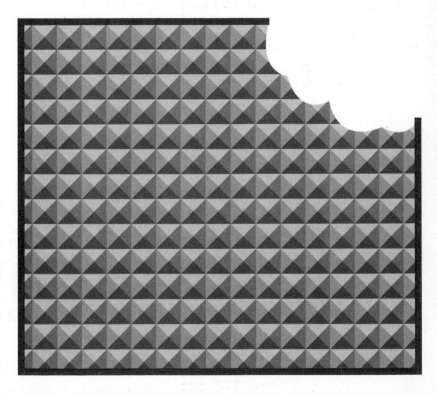

ARE THE **POINTS** ON THE WAFFLE **RAISED** OR ARE THEY **INDENTED?** WHAT DO **YOU** THINK?

TRACK RECORD!

ARE THE **LONG, HORIZONTAL LINES** IN THIS ILLUSTRATION **PARALLEL?**

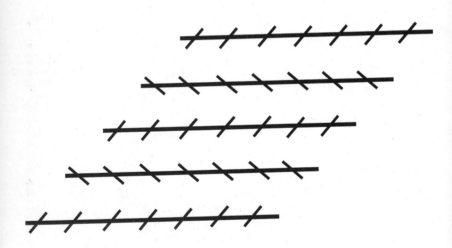

THEY ARE! THE SMALLER **CROSS-LINES** ARE **DISTORTING** THEM!

FELINE FINE!

THE SIGN SAYS, *"THE CAT,"* RIGHT? TAKE A *CLOSER* LOOK. THE *MIDDLE LETTER* ISN'T REALLY AN *H* OR AN *A.* WE SEE IT AS *BOTH* BECAUSE WE *WANT TO!*

STRANGE!

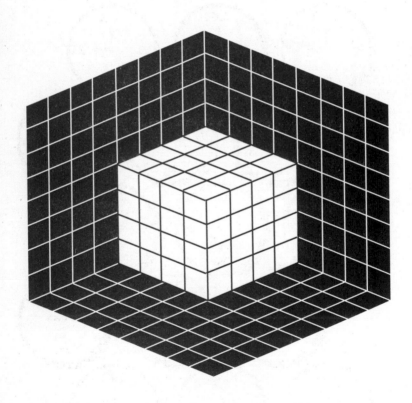

IS THIS A *LITTLE WHITE CUBE* SITTING IN A *CORNER,* OR IS IT A BIG BLACK CUBE WITH A *CORNER CHUNK TAKEN OUT?* YOU DECIDE!

CUCKOO CLOCKS!

WHICH CLOCK IS *WRONG?*

MOST *PEOPLE* WOULD SAY THE *CLOCK* THAT SAYS *10 TO 3* IS *WRONG*...BUT MAYBE IT'S *RIGHT,* AND ALL THE *OTHERS* ARE *WRONG!*

IN THE DISTANCE!

WHICH OF THE **CIRCLES** IS **BIGGER,** THE ONE
ON **TOP** OR THE ONE ON THE **BOTTOM?**
BELIEVE IT OR NOT, THEY'RE THE **SAME SIZE!**

TUNNEL VISION!

THIS IS A *TUNNEL,* RIGHT?   OR IS IT A *CONE?*
STRANGE, BUT IT CAN BE *EITHER!*

CRACK THE CODE!

THERE ARE *SIX LETTERS* HIDDEN IN THESE *DOTS!* CAN YOU SEE WHAT THEY ARE?

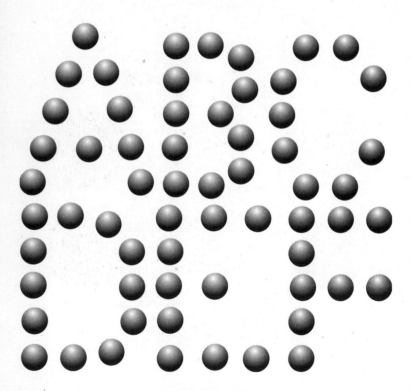

TURN, TURN, TURN!

MOVE THIS PAGE WHILE LOOKING AT THE CIRCLES.

THE SPOKES ON THE OUTER CIRCLES WILL APPEAR TO MOVE!

THAT'S A HONEY!

LOOK CLOSELY AT THIS *HONEYCOMB*.

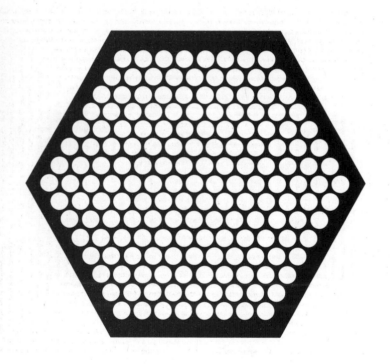

AMAZING!

ARE YOU LOOKING AT THE *TOP* OF A *PYRAMID,* OR
ARE YOU LOOKING *DOWN* A LONG *HALLWAY?*

LET'S MEET UP!

DO THE *DIAGONAL LINES* LINE UP FROM *STRIPE* TO *STRIPE,* OR DO THEY *MISS* EACH OTHER?

DOUBLE TAKE!

Visit
Paris in the
the springtime.

YOU *THINK* IT SAYS, "VISIT PARIS
IN THE SPRINGTIME," *RIGHT?* READ
IT AGAIN, *CAREFULLY* THIS TIME!

I'M BROKEN!

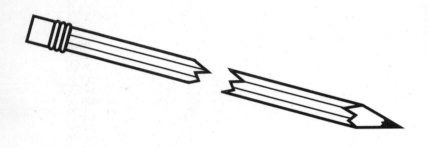

YOU CAN **FIX** THIS **BROKEN** PENCIL! WATCH
THE PENCIL **COME TOGETHER** AS YOU
SLOWLY BRING THE PAGE TO YOUR **NOSE!**

WOW!

DO YOU SEE THE **SIDE** OF A **BEAUTIFUL YOUNG GIRL,** OR THE FACE OF AN **UGLY WOMAN?**

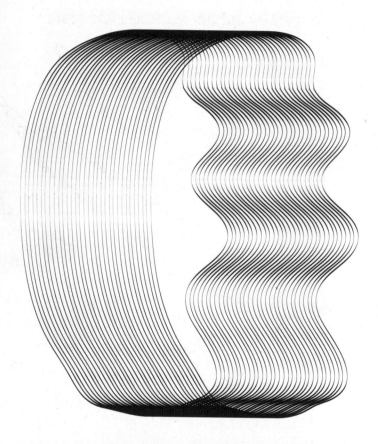

BUG-EYED!

HOW MANY *BUGS* DO YOU *SEE* HERE?

YOE!

EYE OF THE TIGER!

THIS IS A **BUTTERFLY**, BUT IF YOU TURN THE PAGE **UPSIDE DOWN**, WHAT DO YOU SEE?

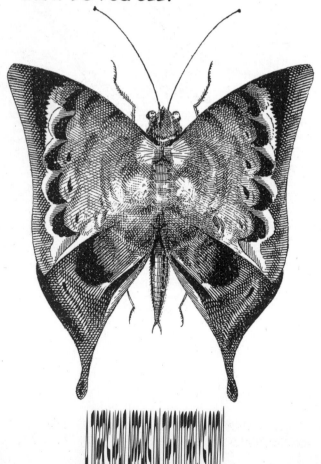

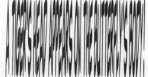

A TIGER'S HEAD APPEARS ON THE BUTTERFLY'S BODY!

ONE-LINER, PART 1!

THIS **DOGGIE** IS MADE UP OF ONE
CONTINUOUS LINE! CHECK IT OUT!

BIRD'S THE WORD!

HELP GUIDE THIS *BIRD* INTO HIS *CAGE* BY
FOCUSING ON THE *DOT* AND BRINGING THE BOOK
CLOSE TO YOUR *FACE.*

ODD BALLS!

DO YOU THINK YOU COULD **BUILD**
THESE **SHELVES?** LOOK AGAIN!
IT'S AN **IMPOSSIBLE FIGURE!**

THERE'S A STAR IN THAR!

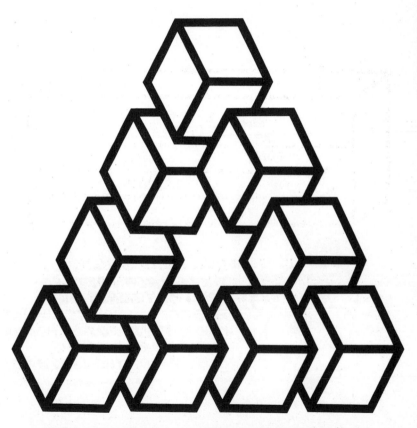

SURE, YOU **SEE** A **STAR** IN THE MIDDLE OF THESE CUBES, BUT IS IT **REALLY** THERE? IT'S ACTUALLY AN **OPEN SPACE!**

SWEET!

COOKIE BOY

THESE **HALF LETTERS** SPELL OUT SOMETHING **TASTY.** CAN YOU TELL WHAT IT IS? **FIND OUT** BY HOLDING A **MIRROR** UP TO THE **BOTTOM** OF THE **LETTERS!**

iNTER-BANG!

IN THE **1970'S,** A DESIGNER CREATED THIS **SYMBOL** AND CALLED IT AN **"INTER-BANG"!** IT'S A CROSS BETWEEN A **QUESTION MARK** AND AN **EXCLAMATION POINT;** YOU KNOW, LIKE WHEN YOUR **PARENTS** SAY TO YOU, "YOU GOT **WHAT** ON YOUR MATH TEST‽"

LEAN ON ME!

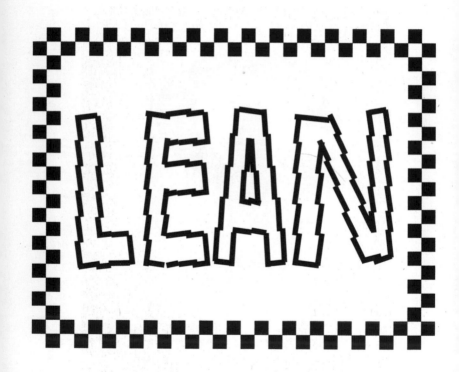

THESE LETTERS *LOOK CROOKED* BUT, *SHOCKINGLY,* THEY'RE *STRAIGHT!*

ALL iS VANiTY!

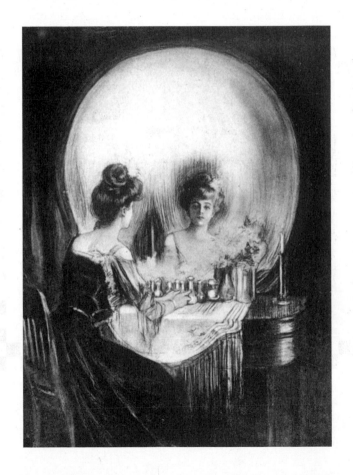

DO YOU SEE A **LADY ADMIRING** HERSELF
IN A **MIRROR** OR DO YOU SEE A **SKULL?**
LOOK **CLOSELY** AND YOU WILL SEE **BOTH!**

WHEELY-DEALY!

HELP THIS *BICYCLIST* GET TO WHERE HE'S GOING! IF YOU *ROCK* THE BOOK *BACK* AND *FORTH,* THE *WHEELS* WILL START TO LOOK LIKE THEY'RE *SPINNING!*

WHISTLER'S COOKIE!

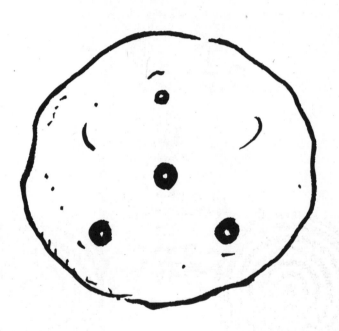

MMMM, THIS COOKIE LOOKS **GOOD!** TURN IT **UPSIDE DOWN** AND IT'LL LOOK EVEN BETTER! IN FACT, IT'LL LOOK LIKE SOMEONE **WHISTLING!**

MORPHO THE MAGICIAN!

HERE'S A NICE PICTURE OF **MORPHO THE MAGICIAN!** TURN IT **UPSIDE DOWN** AND HE'LL PULL A **RABBIT** OUT OF HIS **HAT!**

STAGGERING!

STARE AT THIS **LONG ENOUGH** AND THE **BOXES** START PLAYING **TRICKS** ON YOUR **EYES!**

SWITCH-A-ROO #2!

IS THIS A **MAN** PLAYING THE **BANJO** OR A MAN PLAYING THE **FLUTE?** FLIP THE PAGE TO **FIGURE IT OUT!**

DOGGONE COOL!

THIS IS A ***DACHSHUND*** THROUGH AND THROUGH!

CHECKER OUT!

ARE THE **CREASES** OF **THIS FOLDED CHECKERBOARD** COMING **TOWARD** YOU OR ARE THEY **FOLDED AWAY** FROM YOU?

LOOK AT THIS *BLURRY CIRCLE.* IT FEELS LIKE
YOU'RE LOOKING INTO A *TUNNEL,* DOESN'T IT?

COLOR ME CONFUSED!

SURE, IT **LOOKS** JUST LIKE A **PAINTBRUSH**, BUT **LOOK AGAIN!**

NOW IT'S *PETE THE PAINTER!*

IN THE SHADOWS #2

CREATE YOUR OWN *ILLUSION!* HAVE AN *ADULT* HELP YOU MAKE A *DUCK* APPEAR BY HOLDING YOUR *HANDS* AS SHOWN IN FRONT OF A *STRONG LIGHT* IN A *DARK ROOM!*

SEE SPOTS RUN!

JUST A **BLACK** AND **WHITE GRID**, RIGHT? TAKE A LONGER, *CLOSER LOOK*.

GRAY CIRCLES APPEAR AT THE INTERSECTIONS

BEHIND BARS!

WHICH CIRCLE IS A *DARKER SHADE* OF *GRAY?*

THEY ARE THE *SAME* SHADE OF GRAY! AT THE
RIGHT, THE GRAY *OVERLAPS* THE *BLACK* BARS,
MAKING IT *LIGHTER* IN CONTRAST. AT THE LEFT,
THE GRAY *OVERLAPS* THE *WHITE* BARS, MAKING
IT LOOK *DARKER.*

TALL TALE!

WHO'S _TALLER_, THE MAN ON THE _RIGHT_ OR THE MAN ON THE _LEFT?_

FACE iT!

HAVING TROUBLE *RECOGN-EYE-SING* THESE WORDS? HOLD THE PAGE UP TO A *MIRROR!*

θγθ
wοɿd

BEND THERE!

THIS COLUMN OF CIRCLES LOOKS *CURVED*, RIGHT?

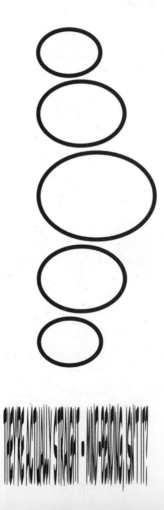

CLOWNING AROUND!

WHICH DISTANCE IS *LONGER* — *1* TO *1* OR *2* TO *2?*
THEY ARE THE *SAME!*

DON'T WORRY, BE HAPPY!

IS THIS TINY ELEPHANT **HAPPY** OR **SAD?** TURN THE PAGE **UPSIDE DOWN.** NOW WHAT DO YOU **THINK?**

TAIL GAZING!

COCK-A-DOODLE-HUH? WHAT'S **WRONG** WITH THE **SHAPE** IN THE ROOSTER'S **TAIL?** IT **LOOKS DISTORTED!**

THREE'S A CROWD!

**WHICH 3 IS THE LARGEST?
WHICH IS THE SMALLEST?**

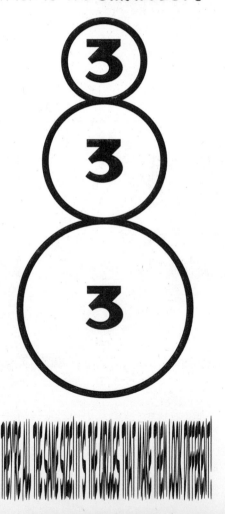

WHAT'S THE ANGLE?

CAN YOU MAKE THIS *IMPOSSIBLE SHAPE* IN SHOP CLASS?

EYE-YIE-YIE!

EYE WONDER... WILL THE *NUMBER* 1 SHAPES FIT IN THE *NUMBER 2* OPEN SPACES?

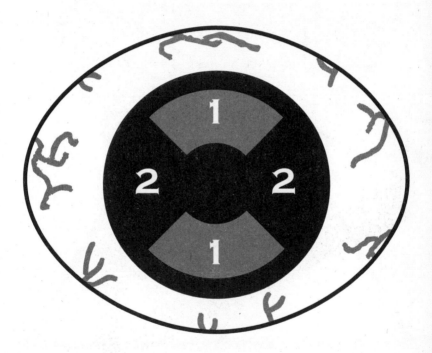

TRi-THiS!

I CAN'T TELL YOU **WHAT** THE POINT IS, BUT I CAN TELL YOU **WHERE** IT IS! THE **WHITE DOT** IS **MIDWAY** BETWEEN THE **TOP** AND **BOTTOM** OF THE BLACK TRIANGLE!

FEAST YOUR EYES!

WHAT DO YOU SEE? **BLACK VASES** OR **WHITE GOBLETS?**

iMPOSSIBLE!

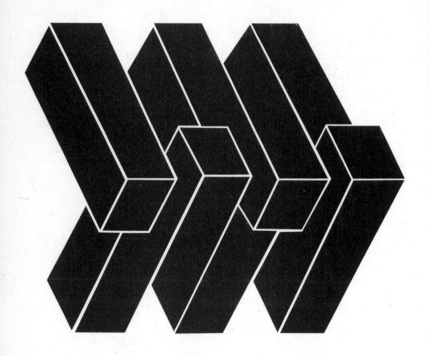

HOW MANY **BLOCKS** DO YOU SEE HERE?
YOU'D BETTER **COUNT AGAIN!** IT'S AN
IMPOSSIBLE SHAPE!

WHAT GOES AROUND . . .

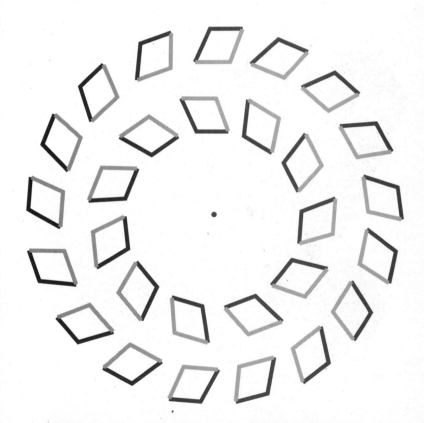

STARE AT THE DOT IN THE **CENTER** OF THE CIRCLE. KEEP LOOKING, AND **MOVE** THE PAGE **TOWARD** AND **AWAY** FROM YOUR HEAD. THE **RINGS** WILL START TO **MOVE!**

STRAIGHTEN UP!

ARE THE VERTICAL LINES *PARALLEL* OR *CURVED?* AMAZINGLY, THEY ARE PARALLEL, BUT THE BLACK AND WHITE BOXES *CONFUSE* YOUR *EYES* AND MAKE YOU THINK OTHERWISE!

SO LONG!

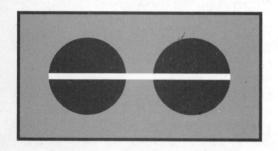

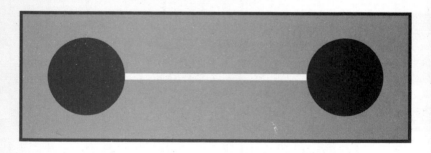

WHICH *WHITE LINE* IS LONGER?
BELIEVE IT OR NOT, THEY ARE
THE *SAME SIZE!*

HORSING AROUND!

GET A LOAD OF THIS **GUY.** TURN HIM
OVER AND HE GETS A LITTLE **HORSE!**

JUST DUCKY!

ARTIST **GEORGE CARLSON** DREW A PAIR OF **DUCKS,** RIGHT? FLIP THE PAGE **UPSIDE DOWN** AND WHAT DO YOU SEE? IT LOOKS LIKE A **CLOWN LYING DOWN!**

SUN FUN!

SO YOU THINK YOU'RE PRETTY *BRIGHT?* DO YOU NOTICE ANYTHING *FUNNY* ABOUT THIS *SUNNY* WORD?

suns

IT'S THE SAME WORD UPSIDE DOWN!

LOOK AT THIS FARMER'S **PITCHFORK.** DOES IT HAVE **TWO PRONGS** OR **THREE?** KEEP **LOOKING,** AND IT'LL KEEP **CHANGING!**

MOVING EXPERIENCES!

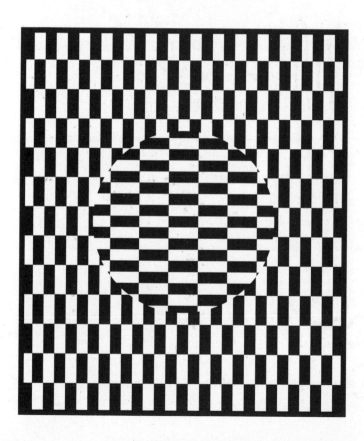

**THIS IS OFF THE *WALL!* LOOK AT THE *CIRCLE*
WHILE *ROCKING* THE PAGE *BACK* AND *FORTH!***

WHAT'S UP DOC?

SURELY THE CARROT ON THE **RIGHT** IS SMALLER THAN THE CARROT ON THE **LEFT!**

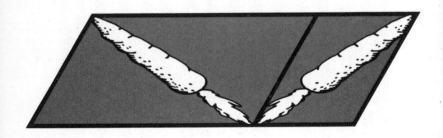

WHAT'S UP DOCK?

WHICH *DISTANCE* IS LONGER — THE DISTANCE FROM *A* TO *B* OR THE DISTANCE FROM *C* TO *D*?

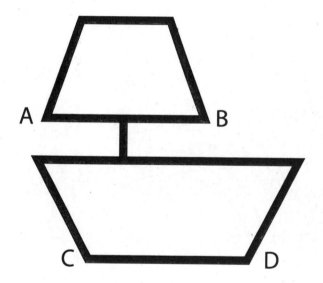

MAGICAL!

IT LOOKS LIKE THERE'S A **THICK WHITE LINE** RUNNING DOWN THE **CENTER** OF THIS **CIRCLE**, DOESN'T IT? AND IT LOOKS LIKE THERE ARE **WHITE DOTS** WHERE THE BLACK LINES **INTERSECT**.

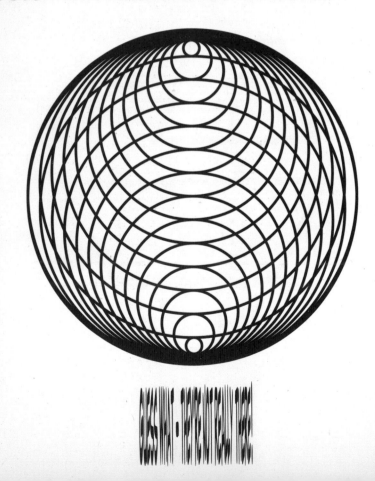

GUESS WHAT - THEY'RE NOT REALLY THERE!

NOTHING DOING!

THOSE AREN'T *JUST* A BUNCH OF *SHAPES* YOU'RE LOOKING AT. TURN THIS PAGE TO THE *SIDE* AND LOOK CLOSELY – YOU'LL SEE A *SECRET MESSAGE.* CAN YOU *READ* WHAT IT SAYS?

SPRING TO MIND!

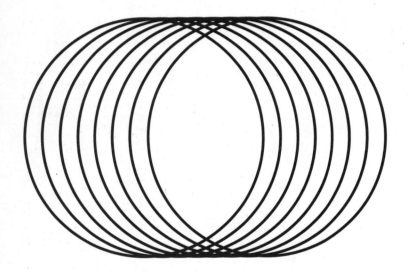

ARE YOU **LOOKING INTO** THIS **SPRING**
FROM THE **LEFT** OR FROM THE **RIGHT?**

OH!

 OH !!!!

MANY YEARS AGO, *OLIVER HERFORD*
DREW THIS CARTOON, ENTITLED, *"THE
FATE OF THE MAN WHO WAS TOO
EASILY SURPRISED."*

RUBBER PENCILS!

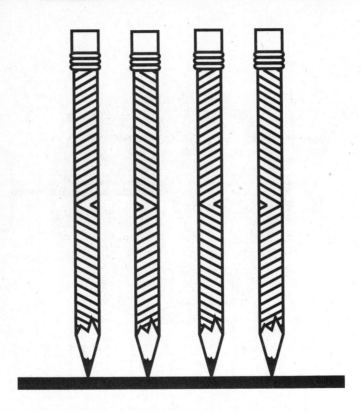

THESE PECULIAR **PENCILS** LOOK LIKE THEY'RE **BENT,** BUT THEY'RE REALLY **PERFECTLY STRAIGHT!**

LOOK-SEE!

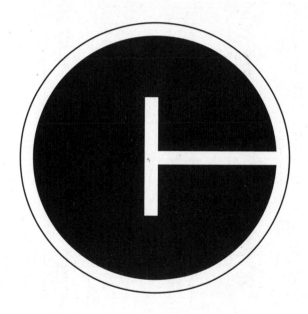

WHAT DO YOU **SEE?** A **CIRCLE** WITH
A **SECTION MISSING** OR THE
LETTER C?

SMOKE & MIRRORS!

· GIRL WITH A CHEESE SANDWICH ·

NAPOLEON CROSSING THE D'LA'WARE

· SUNSET ON THE CANARSIE RIVER ·

· PORTRAIT OF MRS · GRUNDY ·

ARTIST **GEORGE CARLSON** CREATED THIS **MASTERPIECE,** WHICH IS REALLY **FOUR** PICTURES IN **ONE!** FIRST LOOK AT IT FROM THE **BOTTOM,** THEN THE **RIGHT SIDE,** THEN THE **TOP,** AND FINALLY THE **LEFT SIDE!** SEE?

HOT DOG!

HOW MANY *DOGS* ARE ON THIS *PAGE?*

YoE!

ONE - THEY'RE THREE DIFFERENT VIEWS OF THE SAME TWO-TONE DOG!

LOOK AT ME!

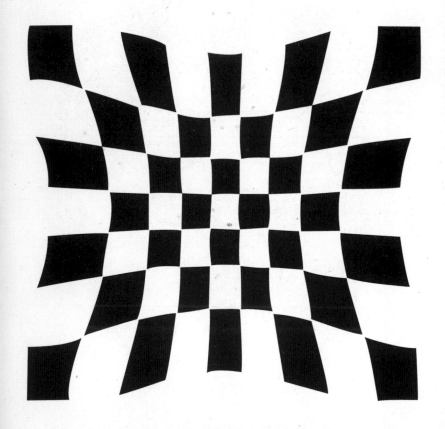

HELP ME MAKE THIS **CURVY** CHECKERBOARD **STRAIGHT!** CLOSE ONE **EYE** AND BRING THE PAGE CLOSE TO THE **OPEN EYE.** IT'S GETTING **STRAIGHTER,** ISN'T IT?

MAN 2 MAN!

WANT TO SEE THIS GUY *LOSE HIS HAIR* AND *GROW A MUSTACHE?* TURN THE PAGE *UPSIDE DOWN* AND YOU WILL!

SEEING SPOTS!

STARE AT THE **SPOTS** ON THE **LEFT PAGE** FOR **30 SECONDS.** THEN LOOK AT THE PICTURE OF **SPOT** ON THE **RIGHT PAGE.** DID YOU SEE WHAT **HAPPENED?** IF NOT, TRY IT **AGAIN!**

YOE!

SUPER SIZES!

WHAT DO THESE *SHAPES* ALL HAVE IN *COMMON?*

CIRCLE AROUND!

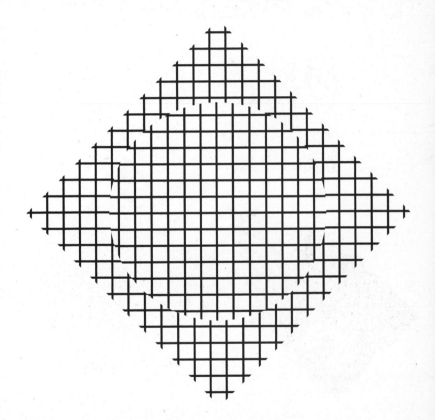

THERE IS NO **CIRCLE** IN THIS **DIAMOND** — ONLY THE **ILLUSION** OF ONE BECAUSE OF THE **LINES!**

WORD UP!

IS THE **BLACK SHAPE** A **"3"** OR A **"W"**? IT WORKS AS **BOTH** TO SPELL OUT **"3 WISHES"**!

ELe-PHUN!

HOW MANY *ELEPHANTS* DO YOU SEE IN THIS *PICTURE?*

IN THE SHADOWS #3

CREATE YOUR OWN *ILLUSION!* HAVE AN *ADULT* HELP YOU MAKE AN *ELEPHANT* APPEAR BY HOLDING YOUR *HANDS* AS SHOWN IN FRONT OF A *STRONG LIGHT* IN A *DARK ROOM!*

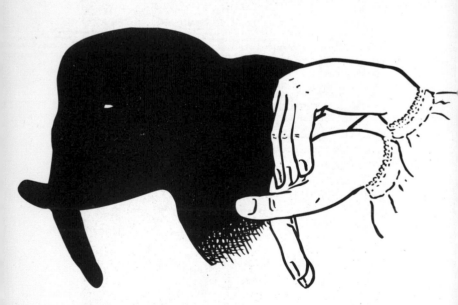

WHAT A TRICK!

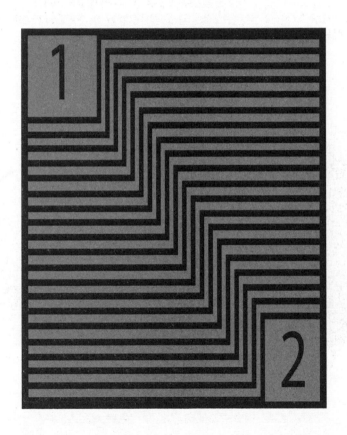

WHICH IS **CLOSER** TO YOU – THE *1* OR THE *2?*
KEEP LOOKING...*YOU'LL SEE* WHAT I *MEAN!*

THE **MIRROR IMAGE** OF THE WORD
"TEACH" IS *"LEARN"!* **AMAZING!**

GET THE POINT?

MOVE THE PAGE **BACK** AND **FORTH,** **LEFT** TO **RIGHT.** WATCH THE **FINGER** **CLOSELY** AND IT WILL **FOLLOW** YOU!

FISHIN' FOR ANSWERS!

WHAT'S THE *HOOK?* NO QUESTION
ABOUT IT, *FELIX THE CAT* MAKES
THE *BEST* OF HIS SITUATION!

WORD UP!

HSEL (mirrored)

WHAT DOES THIS REPRESENT TO *YOU*?

TREE-MENDOUS!

NOW THIS IS **CREEPY.** CAN YOU FIND THE
GHOST OF **NAPOLEON?**

ALL ABOUT U!

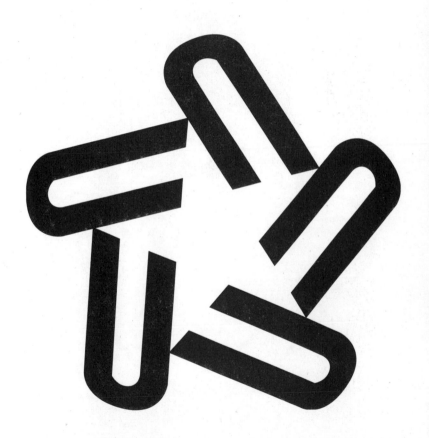

YOUR **MIND** SEES A **STAR** IN THE MIDDLE OF THIS **PATTERN** EVEN THOUGH THERE **ISN'T ONE!**

UPSIE-DOWNSIE!

DOES THIS GUY HAVE **REALLY THICK EYEBROWS** AND A LITTLE **BOW TIE,** OR DOES HE HAVE A **MUSTACHE** AND A **BEARD** AND A **LITTLE HAT?** TURN THE PAGE **UPSIDE DOWN AND** SEE WHAT YOU THINK!

DUDE LOOKS LIKE A DONKEY!

ONLY THE *SHADOW* KNOWS FOR SURE!

MAGIC SQUARE!

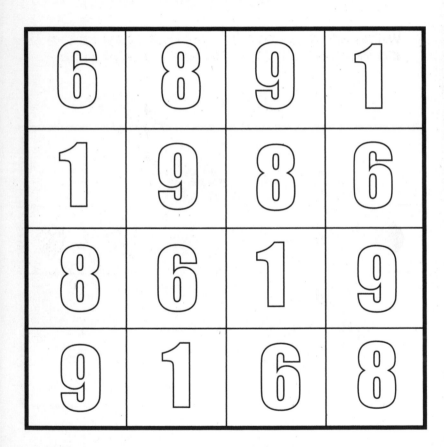

UP OR **DOWN, SIDE** TO **SIDE,** OR **DIAGONAL,** ANYWAY YOU **LOOK** AT IT, THESE ROWS OF **NUMBERS** ADD UP TO **24!**

LiNE EM UP!

WHICH _LINE_ ON TOP OF THE _CIRCLES_ IS THE _CONTINUATION_ OF THE LINE _BELOW_ THEM?

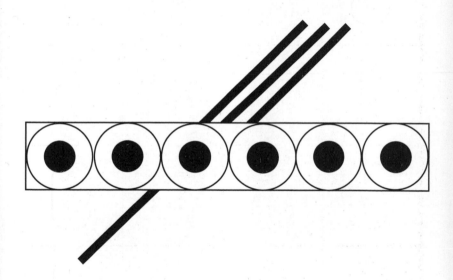

SEEING DOUBLE!

IN THE **DARK,** THIS LADY LOOKS **SUPER-SKINNY!**

BUT WHEN SHE STEPS OUT INTO THE *LIGHT,* WE SEE
THAT SHE'S ACTUALLY *MUCH BIGGER!*

NEVER-ENDING STARES!

HOW *LONG* WOULD IT TAKE YOU TO CLIMB TO THE *TOP* OF THIS *CRAZY STAIRCASE?*

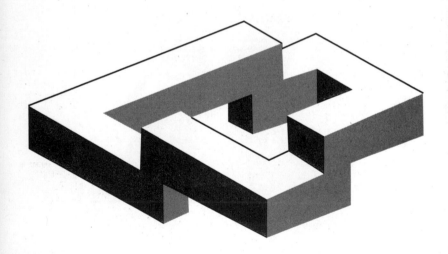

WITH THIS RING!

HOW WOULD YOU PUT ON THIS *RING?* FROM THE *RIGHT* OR FROM THE *LEFT?*

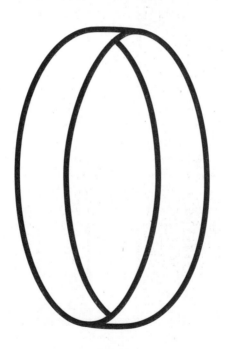

FOOL THE EYE!

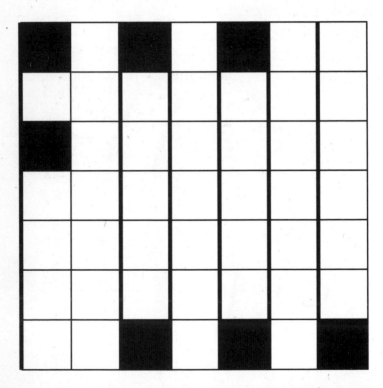

THIS LOOKS JUST LIKE A **BLANK CROSSWORD PUZZLE,** RIGHT? YOU'VE BEEN **FOOLED!** HOLD THE BOOK AT AN **ANGLE** AT **EYE LEVEL,** AND I'LL SPELL IT OUT FOR YOU!

UNCLE SUM!

PRETTY COOL DRAWING OF *UNCLE SAM,* HUH?
LOOK CLOSELY!

YOE!

HIS FACE IS MADE OUT OF THE NUMBERS 1 TO 9!

SMOOCH MOVE!

NOW **HERE'S** A NOTE YOU'D WANT TO GET IN **MATH CLASS!** LOOK AT THIS PAGE **UPSIDE DOWN** IN A **MIRROR.**

SOMETHING'S FISHY HERE!

THIS IS AN *UNUSUAL* WAY TO GET *DRESSED!*

SWITCH-A-ROO #3!

THIS **DUCK** BETTER WATCH OUT! TURN THE PAGE **UPSIDE DOWN** AND YOU'LL SEE A **MONSTER** IN THE WATER!

WORD UP!

WHAT DO THE *MUSKETEERS* SAY?

1 all
all
all
all

ON THE LINE!

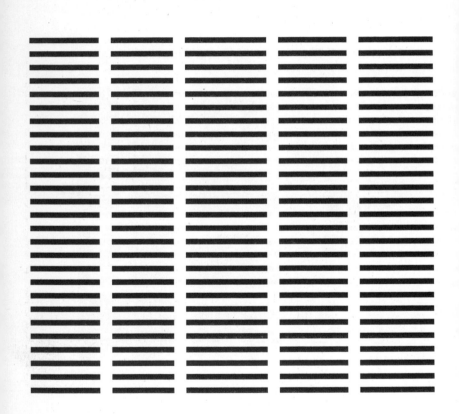

DO YOU SEE THE **LITTLE GRAY CIRCLES** STARTING TO APPEAR IN THE **WHITE VERTICAL LINES?** LOOK A LITTLE **LONGER** AND YOU WILL.

WING IT!

ARE THESE **THREE AIRPLANES** FACING IN THE **SAME DIRECTION?** LOOK CLOSELY! THEY ARE **NOT!**

HERE'S LOOKING AT U!

IS THIS **MAN** LOOKING AT THE **BIRD** OR THE **CAT**?
LOOK CLOSELY AT HIS **EYES.** THEY COULD BE
LOOKING EITHER **UP** OR **DOWN!**

CRAZY VASE!

LOOK AT THIS *VASE* – THE LINES *AREN'T* REALLY *CONNECTED!* HOW IS THE WATER *STAYING INSIDE?*

DOUBLE OR NOTHING!

DO **BUNNIES QUACK?** TURN
THE PICTURE AND **LOOK AGAIN!**

CROSS MY HEART!

IS THIS CROSS *INSIDE* THE BOX, OR IS IT *OUTSIDE?*
IT'S A *SILLY, IMPOSSIBLE* FIGURE!

OME

TWO

WANT TO HAVE SOME *FUN?*
START BY LOOKING AT *ONE,*
TURN IT *UPSIDE DOWN,*
NOW *TWO'S* IN *TOWN.*

TURN IT TO THE *RIGHT*
AND *THREE* IS WHAT YOU'LL *SEE.*
THEN *UPSIDE DOWN* ONCE *MORE*
AND YOU'LL SEE *FOUR!*

THREE'S COMPANY!

HOW MANY *LADIES* DO YOU SEE IN THIS *PICTURE?*
ONE – THE ONE IN THE *MIDDLE.* EVERYTHING ELSE
IS JUST *TREES* IN THE *BACKGROUND!*

iT'S HiP TO BE SQUARE!

ARE YOU *LOOKING THROUGH* THESE SQUARES FROM THE *LEFT* OR FROM THE *RIGHT?* ARE YOU *SURE?*

WAVY-GRAVY!

THOSE ARE SOME *CROOKED BLACK LINES,* AREN'T THEY? THERE ARE *NOT!* THEY ARE *STRAIGHT!* IT'S THAT *BACKGROUND* THAT MAKES THEM LOOK *BENT!*

iNSIDE OUT!

WHICH GRAY CIRCLE IS *SMALLER?*

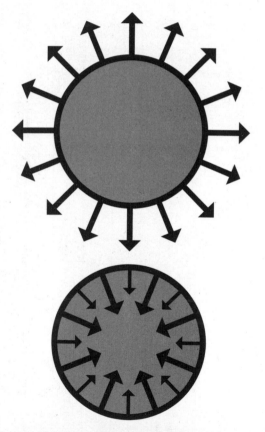

THEY'RE THE *SAME SIZE,* BUT
THE *OUTWARD-POINTING
ARROWS* MAKE THE *TOP CIRCLE*
LOOK *BIGGER!*

FLOWER POWER!

WHICH OF THE *TWO DOTS* IS IN THE *CENTER*?

CHOP FOOEY!

WHICH FORTUNE COOKIE IS *BIGGER?*

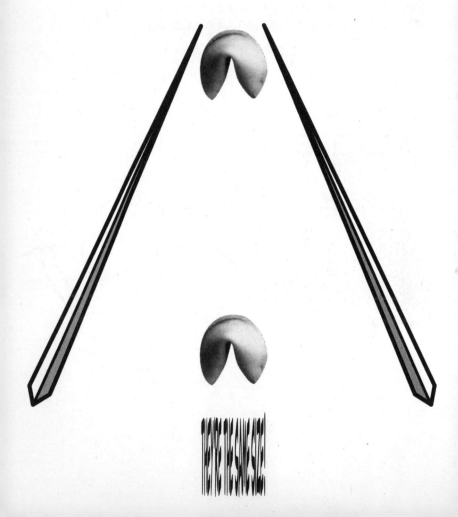

THEY'RE THE SAME SIZE!

iN THE SHADOWS #4

CREATE YOUR OWN *ILLUSION!* HAVE AN *ADULT* HELP YOU MAKE A *GOAT* APPEAR BY HOLDING YOUR *HANDS* AS SHOWN IN FRONT OF A *STRONG LIGHT* IN A *DARK ROOM!*

BETWEEN THE LINES!

WHICH GRAY LINE IS *LONGER?*

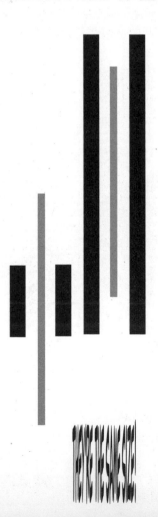

THEY'RE THE SAME SIZE!

iN STiTCHES!

YOU DID ALRIGHT WITH *TWO HIDDEN MESSAGES;* NOW LET'S SEE HOW YOU DO WITH *THREE!*

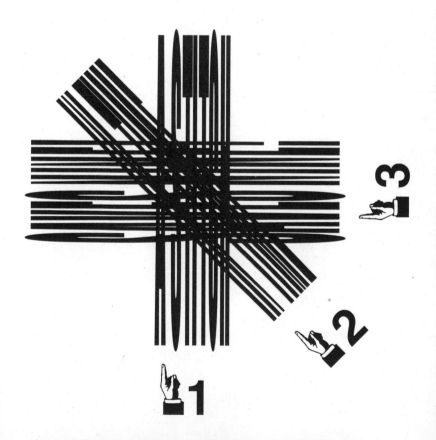

DID YOU *GET* IT? IT SAYS, *"A STITCH IN TIME SAVES NINE!"*

ART FOR ART'S SAKE!

THIS IS MY PAL **ART.** HE'S AN **ARTIST,**
AND **HE'S CREATED ART.** LOOK
CLOSELY AT HIS **SCULPTURE!**

REPEAT AFTER ME!

CAN YOU CATCH THE *MISTAKE* IN THIS *SENTENCE?*

> # OVER THE RIVER AND THROUGH THE THE WOODS

Sincerely Yours,

Woodrow Wilson

PEOPLE PERSON!

WOODROW WILSON WAS A **PEOPLE PERSON.** AT LEAST HE WAS IN THIS **PICTURE!** THIS **PORTRAIT** IS MADE UP OF **HUNDREDS** OF **PEOPLE!**

HERE IS A **CLOSE-UP** OF HIS **CHIN!**

COUNT UP, COUNT DOWN!

HOW MANY *3-D CUBES* DO YOU SEE HERE?

ONE-LINER, PART 2!

THIS *OSTRICH* IS MADE UP OF *ONE CONTINUOUS LINE!*

SEEING SPOTS!

ARE THE *STRIPES* IN ALL THESE CIRCLES *HORIZONTAL? YES!*

iT'S AN . . .

WELL, *WHAT IS IT?* LOOK *CLOSELY!*

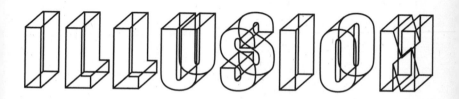

ILLUSION

WHAT'S THE POINT?

WHICH **PENCIL** DO YOU THINK IS **LONGER?**

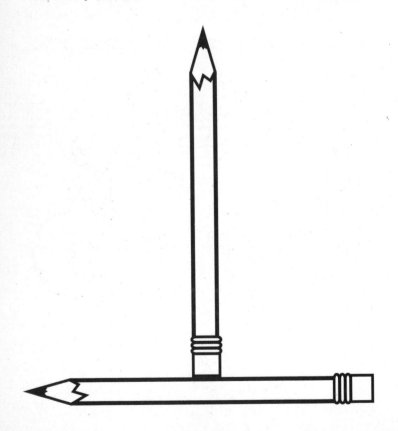

EVEN THOUGH THE **VERTICAL** ONE LOOKS **LONGER,**
THEY ARE **BOTH** THE **SAME SIZE!**

WHAT DO YOU NOSE!

PUT A **MIRROR** ON THE DOTTED LINE, AND **LOOK** INTO IT FROM THE **LEFT!**

THIS GUY'S GOING **CROSS-EYED** LOOKING AT THE **FLY** ON HIS **NOSE!**

THiNK NeGATiVe #1!

STARE AT THIS *NEGATIVE PICTURE* OF *CHARLIE CHAPLIN* FOR *30 SECONDS.* THEN LOOK AT THE *BLANK PAGE* ON THE RIGHT.

YOU'LL SEE THE *CORRECT* IMAGE *APPEAR* BEFORE YOUR *EYES!*

THAT CIRCLE SURE IS **BENT OUT OF SHAPE,** ISN'T IT?

NO! IT'S A PERFECTLY **ROUND CIRCLE!** THE **LINES** BEHIND IT MAKE IT APPEAR **DISTORTED!**

MAKE A SCENE!

NOTICE ANYTHING **EXTRA** IN THIS **SEASIDE SCENE?** DOESN'T IT LOOK LIKE THERE'S A **MAN LYING DOWN** RIGHT IN THE **MIDDLE** OF IT?

RASPBERRIES!

HOW MANY *TONGUES* DO YOU SEE?

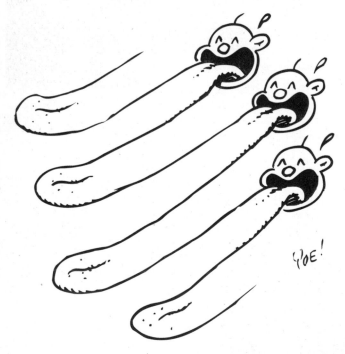

CAREFUL! DON'T GET *LICKED* BY THIS *TRICK!*

AMAZING!

WHOA! IS THIS SHAPE COMING **TOWARD YOU,** OR IS IT GOING **AWAY FROM YOU?** BEATS ME!

YOU ARE GETTING SLEEPY!

ISN'T IT **COOL** HOW IT LOOKS AS THOUGH THERE ARE **SHADOWS** AROUND THE **CENTER CIRCLE**, EVEN THOUGH **THERE AREN'T ANY?**

SCENE DOUBLE!

LOOK AT THIS PAGE, THEN **TURN** IT TO THE **RIGHT** AND LOOK AT IT **AGAIN.** DO YOU SEE A **BEARDED MAN** OR A **VILLAGE SCENE?**

UNBELIEVABLE!

HOW CAN THIS BE? ANOTHER
IMPOSSIBLE SHAPE!

CHECK IT OUT!

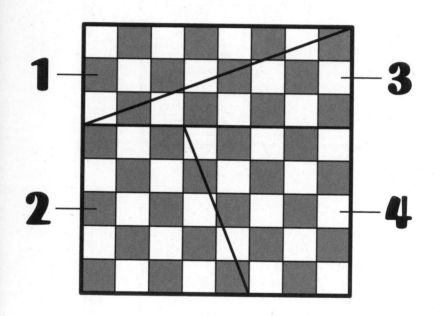

THIS IS **WEIRD!** IF YOU **CUT** THIS **SQUARE** ON
THE **LINES** AND **REARRANGE** IT – LIKE THE
ONE ON THE RIGHT PAGE – IT GOES FROM HAVING
64 SQUARES TO HAVING **65!**

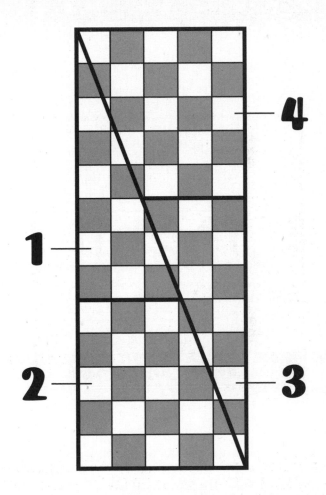

YOU DO THE MATH!

Mathematics

ANY WAY YOU **LOOK** AT IT, THIS PAGE IS ALL ABOUT **MATHEMATICS!** THE WORD'S THE SAME **UPSIDE DOWN!**

LOOK iNTO MY EYES!

ROCK THE BOOK *BACK* AND *FORTH* AND THE
ALIEN'S EYES WILL *SPIN*. OUT OF THIS *WORLD!*

SWITCH-A-ROO #4!

A **PEACEFUL PIG** WADING IN A **SWAMP,** OR THE UNDERSIDE OF A **FIERCE SHARK?** TURN THE PAGE **OVER** AND **LOOK CLOSELY!**

ONE-LINER, PART 3!

THIS *DUCK* IS MADE UP OF *ONE CONTINUOUS LINE!*

LOOK-SEE!

THERE'S NOT A **SQUARE** AND THERE ARE NO **CIRCLES** IN THIS PICTURE! YOUR MIND ONLY **IMPLIES** THAT THERE ARE!

SEEING THINGS!

THOSE LINES LOOK *WAVY,* DON'T THEY?

THEY'RE STRAIGHT! THE CIRCLES MAKE THEM LOOK CURVED!

THiNK NeGATiVe #2!

STARE AT THIS NEGATIVE PICTURE OF
ABRAHAM LINCOLN FOR 30 SECONDS,
THEN LOOK AT THE BLANK PAGE ON THE RIGHT.

YOU'LL SEE THE CORRECT IMAGE
APPEAR BEFORE YOUR EYES!

FARM OUT!

LOOK AT THIS PICTURE TO SEE MY PAL **FARMER BILL.** WHERE IS HIS **FAVORITE COW, BESSIE?** TURN THE PAGE **UPSIDE DOWN** TO FIND HER!

GET MY GOAT!

THIS LADY IS **PRETTY** UNTIL YOU TURN HER **UPSIDE DOWN**, NOW SHE LOOKS LIKE A **GOAT!**

WORD UP!

WHAT DOES *THIS* REPRESENT?

→ LINE
LINE
LINE
LINE

THAT'S NUTS!

THIS IS NO *ORDINARY SQUIRREL!* LOOK CLOSELY!

WHAT TH'?!

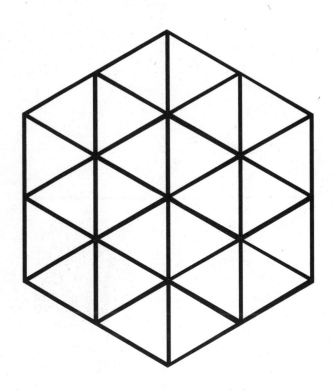

IS THIS JUST A *BUNCH* OF *LINES* OR A *CUBE?*

EEEEEEEEK!

SHE LOOKS PRETTY *MEAN!* I LIKED IT
BETTER WHEN THERE WAS JUST A *MOUSE!*

A, B, C, DOUBLE!

EITHER WAY YOU **LOOK AT** IT —
BACKWARD OR **FORWARD** — THESE
ARE THE **LETTERS** OF THE **ALPHABET!**

© Scott Kim; visit www.scottkim.com

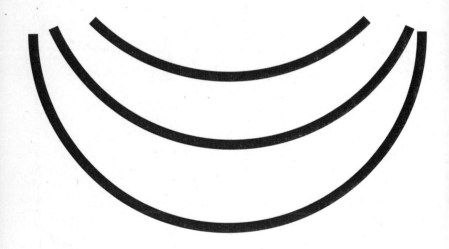

SMiLE!

IT DOESN'T LOOK LIKE IT, BUT THESE *THREE CURVED LINES* CAN MAKE A *PERFECT CIRCLE!*

SAY CHEESE!

WHAT DO *YOU* SEE:

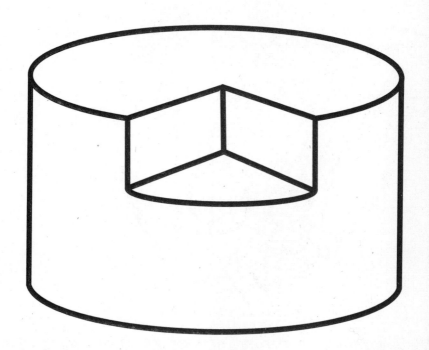

A *CHUNK* OF *CHEESE FLOATING,* OR A *BLOCK* OF *CHEESE* WITH A PIECE *CUT OUT?*

2 BITS!

YOE!

HOLD A *MIRROR* ALONG THE *DOTTED LINE*. IF YOU LOOK *ONE WAY*, THE MAN IS *BEARDED*, IF YOU LOOK THE *OTHER WAY*, HE'S *CLEAN-SHAVEN!*

THAT'S TWEET!

A *BELL* OR *TWO BIRDS* FACING EACH OTHER?

HOLEY-MOLEY!

WATCH YOUR STEP

THIS IS ONE *DEEP MESSAGE!* DON'T THESE *LETTERS* LOOK LIKE *HOLES?*

GOING BATTY!

THE **HORIZONTAL** BAT IS **LONGER** THAN THE **VERTICAL** ONE, RIGHT?

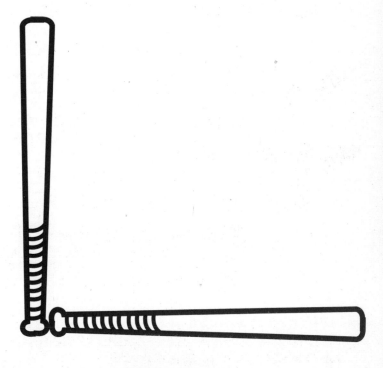

ALPHABET SOUP!

CAN YOU FIND **ALL** THE **LETTERS** OF THE **ALPHABET** IN THIS **DESIGN?** TRUST ME, **THEY'RE IN THERE!**

SEEING THINGS!

LOOK AT THE **CENTER** OF THIS **CIRCLE** – THE **LINES** SEEM TO **BEND INWARD.** AND EVEN THOUGH IT'S ONLY **BLACK** AND **WHITE,** SOME PEOPLE SEE THE COLOR **YELLOW!**

USE YOUR CENTS!

DO YOU THINK YOU COULD FIT A **PENNY** ON THE **TOP** OF THIS **TABLE?** GRAB ONE AND **SEE!**

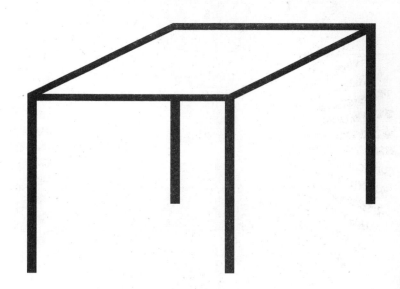

WORD UP!

WHAT DOES *THIS* REPRESENT TO YOU?

SWITCH-A-ROO #6!

IS THIS ATHLETE *JUMPING* FOR THE
BALL OR IS HE *DIVING* FOR IT? FLIP
THE *PAGE* AND *LOOK AGAIN!*

MYSTIFYING!

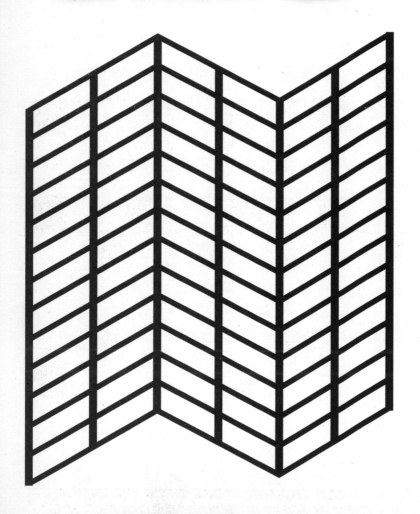

ARE THESE CREASES **POINTING UP,** OR
ARE THEY **FOLDED DOWN?**

ZAP IT!

ARE THESE *HORIZONTAL* LINES *PARALLEL* OR *CROOKED?* THEY'RE *PARALLEL!* IT'S THE PLACEMENT OF THE *BLACK SQUARES* THAT MAKES THEM LOOK *SLANTED!*

A REAL YAWNER!

THIS **GUY** BETTER **WATCH OUT!** IF YOU **LOOK** AT THE **PICTURE** WHILE BRINGING THE BOOK **TOWARD** YOUR **FACE,** HE'S GOING TO **SWALLOW** THAT **BUG!**

YOE!

GIVE ME AN H!

WHAT DO YOU *SEE* HERE? *TWO ARROWS* OR THE *LETTER H?*

KING OF QUEENS!

IS THIS A *HAPPY QUEEN* OR A *GRUMPY KING?*
TURN THE PAGE *UPSIDE DOWN* AND LOOK *AGAIN!*

DID YOU SEE THAT!

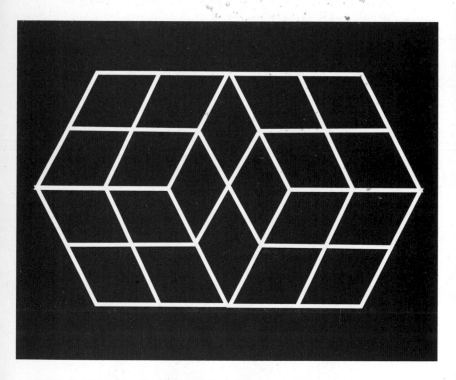

HOW MANY *3-D CUBES* DO YOU SEE? SOMETIMES
YOU SEE *ONE,* SOMETIMES YOU SEE *TWO,* AND
SOMETIMES YOU DON'T SEE *ANY!*

2 THE POINT!

HOLD THIS **PAGE** AT **EYE LEVEL** AND LOOK **ACROSS** IT. AS YOU **GAZE,** YOU'LL SEE A **THIRD SWORD!**

EAGLE UNCLE!

THIS **PATRIOTIC PICTURE** IS MORE THAN JUST AN **AMERICAN EAGLE!** FLIP IT OVER AND SAY HI TO **UNCLE SAM!**

READ MY BLIPS!

READ THE FOLLOWING **PARAGRAPH:**

Something is really wrong with
with this paragraph. Can you see
see it? No? That's because your
your mind sometimes plays tricks
tricks on you and you see what
what you want to, instead of
of what's really on the page!

SO DID YOU **CATCH** WHAT'S WRONG WITH IT?
THE **LAST WORD** OF EACH **LINE** IS REPEATED
AT THE BEGINNING OF THE **NEXT LINE!**

ON TARGET!

WHICH IS *THICKER:* THE *INNER BLACK CIRCLE,* THE *WHITE CIRCLE,* OR THE *OUTER BLACK CIRCLE?* GUESS WHAT? THEY'RE ALL THE *SAME THICKNESS!*

SWITCH-A-ROO #7!

BIRDS OR **RHINOS?** TURN THE PAGE
UPSIDE DOWN TO DECIDE!

LOOKS LIKE A LADY!

STARE AT THE **PICTURE** OF THE **STATUE OF LIBERTY** FOR **30 SECONDS.** THEN LOOK AT THE **BLANK PAGE** ON THE RIGHT.

YOU'LL SEE THE **REVERSE IMAGE** APPEAR BEFORE YOUR **EYES!**

WHAT DOES THIS **REPRESENT** TO YOU?

ALL

ALL **GOOD GUY** **ALL**

ALL

OVERLAP!

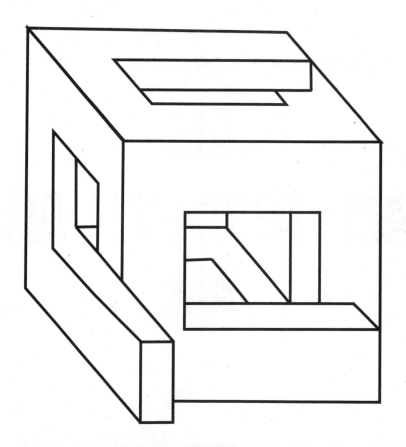

THIS IS ONE **CRAZY CUBE!** IT'S ANOTHER ONE OF THOSE **IMPOSSIBLE FIGURES!**

DOT'S AMAZING!

WHICH **SEGMENT** OF THE **ARROW** IS **BIGGER** – A OR B?

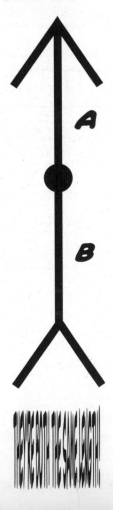

FOUR KICKS!

OKAY, OKAY, SO YOU MASTERED **THREE HIDDEN MESSAGES.** NOW LET'S SEE HOW YOU DO WITH **FOUR!** CAN YOU SEE WHAT IT **SAYS?**

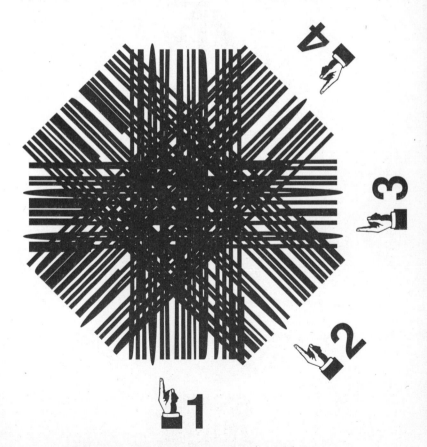

IT'S THE STORY OF **"JACK AND JILL"**!

COCK-A-DOODLE DOO!

CHECK OUT THIS *MAN'S SHADOW!*

FACE FACTS!

ARE THESE *AMAZING ACROBATS* OR WHAT?
TURN THIS PAGE *UPSIDE DOWN* AND THE
ACROBATS FORM A *FACE!*

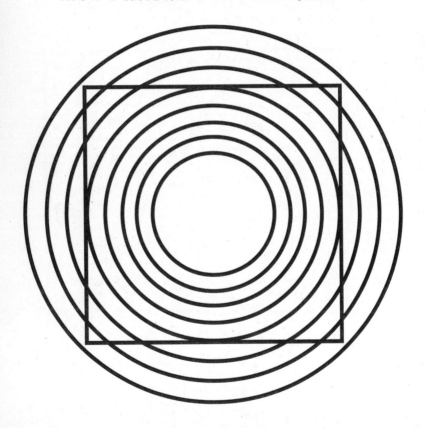

STAR SEARCH!

ARE YOU A *STAR* OR A *SQUARE?*

UNREAL!

NOTICE ANYTHING *ODD* ABOUT THIS *PORTRAIT* OF *NAPOLEON?* IT'S MADE UP OF *BATTLE SCENES* AND *PICTURES* OF HIS *ARMY!*

BEYOND BELIEF!

THIS IS A **CLASSIC ILLUSION!** WHICH LINE IS **LONGER?**

¡IT'S A MYSTERY!

ARE THE *DIAGONAL BLACK LINES* REALLY *BENT?*

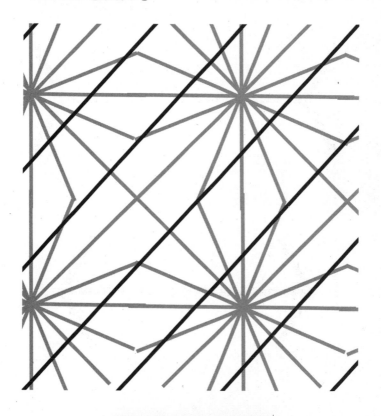

WORD UP!

WHAT DOES THIS *REPRESENT* TO YOU?

TI BACK ME

SWITCH-A-ROO #8!

IS THIS GUY *LEANING* OVER A *FENCE* OR IS HE *DROWNING* BY A *DOCK?* FLIP THE PAGE AND YOU'LL *SEE!*

BiG DEAL!

WHICH *SQUARE* IS *BIGGER?*

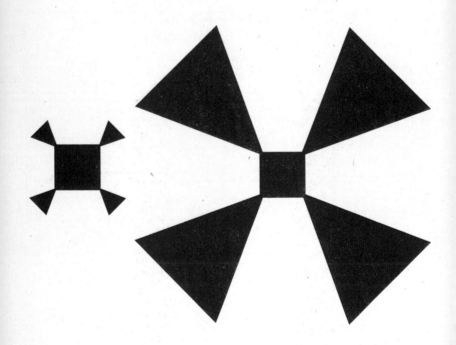

THEY ARE REALLY THE *SAME SIZE!* THE SIZES OF THE *TRIANGLES* MAKE THE ONE ON THE LEFT LOOK *BIGGER!*

FOOL THE EYE!

ARE THESE STRIPED POLES
STRAIGHT OR *SLANTED?*

i CAN'T BELIEVE MY EYES!

WHICH GRAY AREA IS *DARKER?*

IT'S *CRAZY* BUT THE TWO *GRAYS* IN THIS *FIGURE* ARE THE EXACT *SAME SHADE!*

MISSING PERSONS!

THESE **RANDOM, BLURRY DOTS** SURE LOOK LIKE **SOMEONE...**

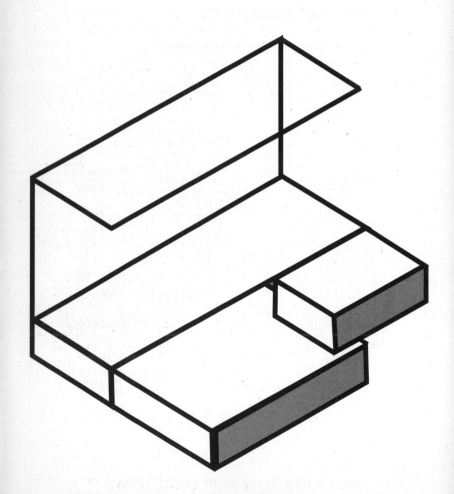

ANOTHER **KOOKY IMPOSSIBLE FIGURE!**

OH BABY!

HOW MANY *BABIES* DO YOU SEE HERE?
LOOK AT IT FROM *EVERY DIRECTION.*
YOU MIGHT BE *SURPRISED!*

ARE THERE *THREE? SIX? NINE?*

TRi & COMPARE!

WHICH *CENTER TRIANGLE* IS *SMALLER*, THE ONE ON THE *LEFT* OR THE ONE ON THE *RIGHT?*

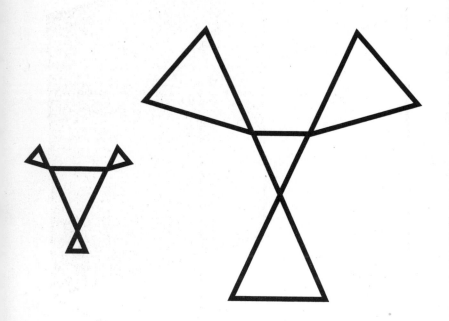

THAT'S SO CUBE!

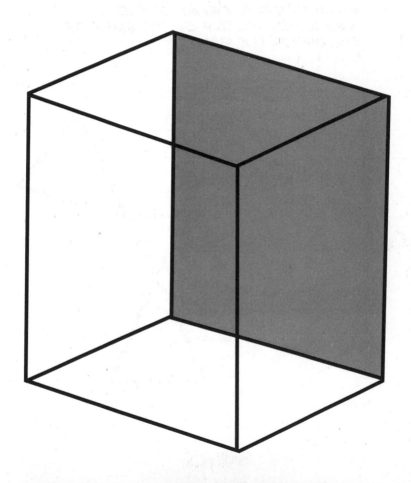

WHICH PART OF THE *BOX* IS *GRAY?* IS IT THE *BACK WALL?* THE *TOP?* THE *INSIDE?* KEEP LOOKING, AND IT'LL *KEEP CHANGING!*

SAY WHAT?

THAT'S ONE **CROOKED TRIANGLE,** ISN'T IT?

EYE-POPPING!

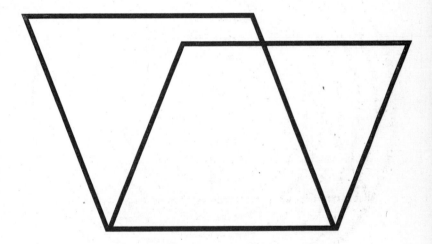

IS THIS *FOLDED PIECE* OF *PAPER*
FACING *LEFT* OR IS IT FACING *RIGHT?*

SWITCH-A-ROO #9!

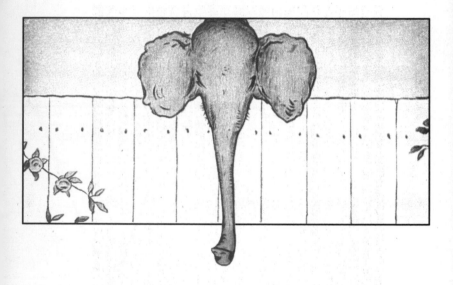

AN **ELEPHANT** PEEKING OVER A **FENCE** OR AN **OSTRICH** STANDING IN FRONT OF A **FENCE?** TURN THE PAGE OVER AND **DECIDE!**

BREAK THE LINES!

CAN YOU SEE THE *BLACK DOTS* WHERE THE *WHITE LINES* INTERSECT?

IS THIS SHAPE *FOUR ARROWS* OR A *DIAMOND* WITH *FOUR SMALL SQUARES* IN IT?

AND HOW ABOUT THIS ONE... **FOUR BLACK ARROWS** OR A **WHITE X** IN A **BOX?**

DiD YOU SEE THAT?

WHAT DO THESE **RANDOM SHAPES** MAKE YOU THINK OF?

WORD UP!

WHAT DOES *THIS* REPRESENT TO YOU?

track

HEE, HEE!

THE *FUNNY SIDE* OF *OPTICAL ILLUSIONS* BY GENIUS CARTOONIST *HARVEY KURTZMAN!*

BiG DEAL!

WHICH *CIRCLE* IS *BIGGER?*

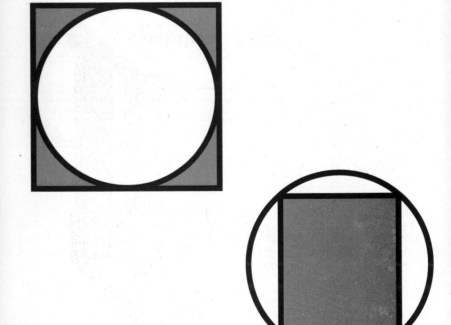

THEY ARE THE *SAME,* IT'S THE POSITION OF THE *SQUARES* THAT MAKE THEM LOOK *DIFFERENT!*

WHOA!

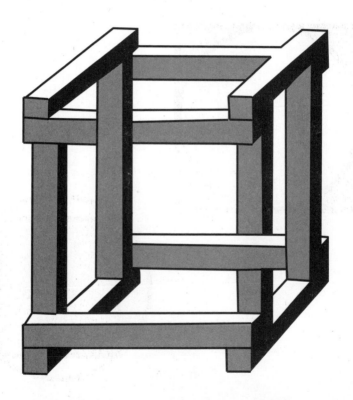

WOW! WHAT IS THAT? THIS **IMPOSSIBLE FIGURE** IS MAKING MY **HEAD HURT!**

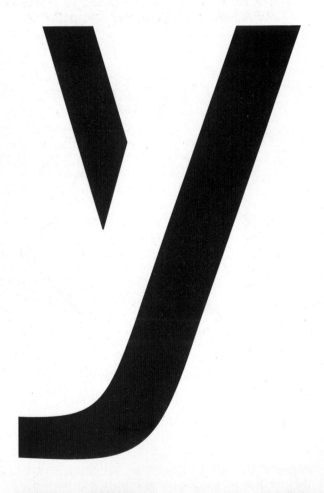

IS IT JUST A **COUPLE** OF **BLACK LINES,**
OR A **3-D LETTER Y?**

SO WHAT DO *YOU* THINK: IS THIS A *PERFECT SQUARE* OR *NOT?*

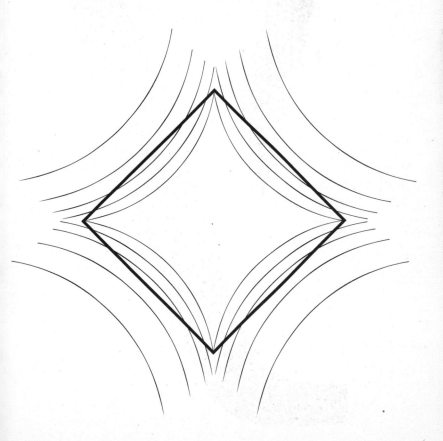

THE *BENT LINES* MAKE ITS *SIDES* LOOK *CURVED,* BUT THEY ARE *PERFECTLY STRAIGHT!*

STARE DOWN!

IF YOU *STARE* AT THIS *PATTERN* LONG ENOUGH, YOU'LL START TO SEE *BLACK DIAGONAL LINES* BETWEEN THE *SQUARES* — EVEN THOUGH THEY'RE *NOT THERE!*

THINK IN/OUTSIDE THE BOX!

IS THE *GRAY DOT* ON THE *OUTSIDE* OF THE *BOX* OR IS IT *INSIDE?*

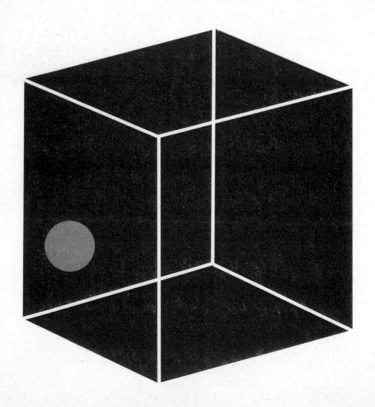

MULE NEVER GUESS!

***MULE* OR *MAN*?** TURN THE PAGE *UPSIDE DOWN*
AND YOU JUST MIGHT *CHANGE* YOUR *MIND!*

GRAY AREA!

IS THE *GRAY AREA* ON THE LEFT *BIGGER* THAN THE *BLACK AREA* ON THE *RIGHT?*

HYPNOTIC!

LOOK AT THIS *CIRCLE* AS YOU *ROTATE* THE *PAGE.*

GRID AND BEAR IT!

DO YOU SEE THE **GRAY DOTS** WHERE THE **LINES INTERSECT?**

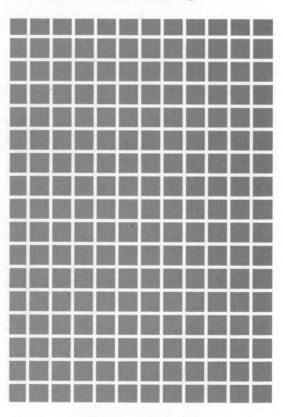

THE *SAME PRINCIPLE* WORKS *HERE!*

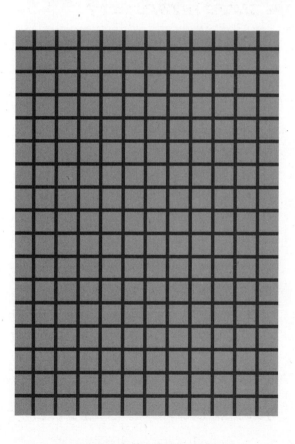

LINE 'EM UP!

DO THE *ARCHES* ON THE LEFT *MATCH UP* WITH THE *ARCHES* ON THE *RIGHT?*

BOOK 'EM!

ARE YOU LOOKING AT THE _COVERS_ OF A _BOOK_ OR THE _PAGES INSIDE?_

FUNNY PAGES!

FOLLOWING THE **ARROWS**, READ THIS **COMIC** OVER THE NEXT **SIX PAGES;** THEN TURN THE BOOK **UPSIDE DOWN** AND KEEP ON **READING** ... YOU'LL END UP **BACK** TO THIS **PAGE!**

S
T
A
R
T

 Both on shore, she gets scolded all the way home. *(The end!)*

 Muffaroo warns Lovekins not to go near the water.

But she does go and alarms a nice lady.
(Go to the next page!)

3 By falling off the embarkment.

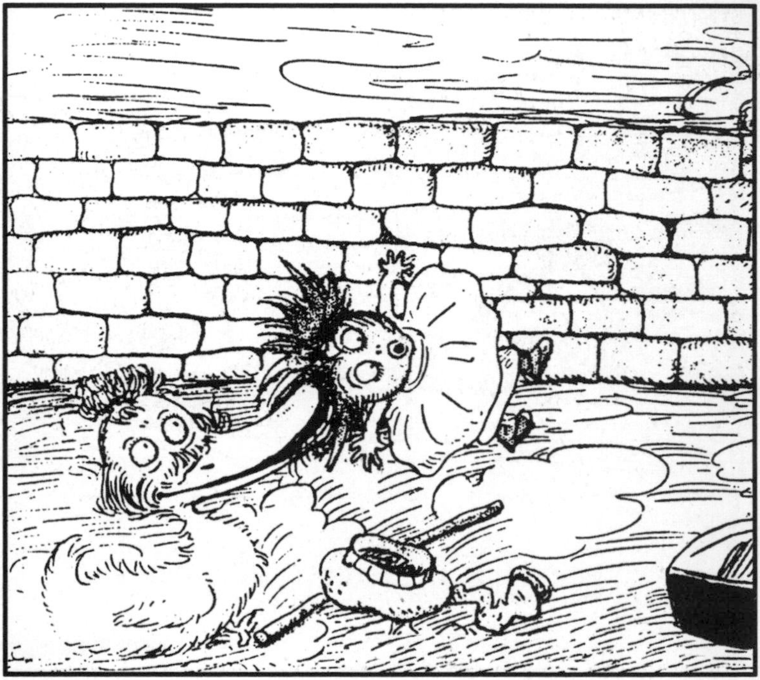

10 And bites Little Lady Lovekins.

(Go to the next page!)

Old Man Muffaroo brings a boat.

(Go to the next page!)

8 All seemed well.

(Go to the next page!)

⬅

5 And throws it to Little Lady Lovekins.

➡

And a big wave tosses her into the boat.

6 The boat strikes the water with a splash.
(Turn the page upside down now!)

HiDE N' SEEK!

WHEN THESE **CATS** SWITCH **PLACES,** IT LOOKS LIKE THEY **DISAPPEAR!**

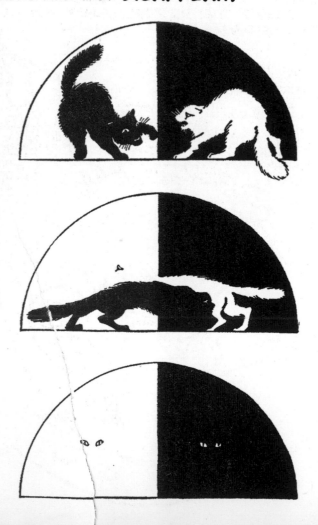

COVER YOUR MOUTH!

HOW MANY **MOUTHS** DO YOU **SEE** IN THIS
PICTURE? HOW MANY **TONGUES** DO YOU **SEE?**
ARE YOU **SURE** THEY'RE **TONGUES?** MAYBE
THEY'RE JUST **HILLS!**

IT'S A BABY!

THIS **NEW BRIDE** IS DREAMING OF **HAVING**
A **BABY** SOMEDAY!

SIZE 'EM UP!

WHICH OF THESE **HAPPY FELLAS** IS THE **SMALLEST?**

USE YOURS!

BRAIN

CAN YOU *READ* THIS *WORD?*

STAIRY EYED!

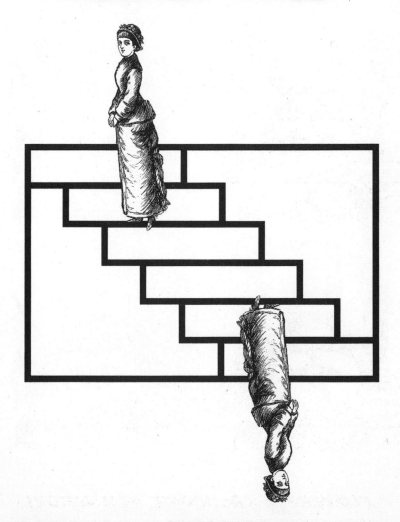

WHICH WAY DO THE **STAIRS** GO? TURN THE PAGE
UPSIDE DOWN AND THEN **DECIDE!**

DOUBLE FUN!

IS THIS A *SAD YOUNG WOMAN* OR A *TOOTHLESS OLD LADY?* TURN THE PAGE *UPSIDE DOWN,* THEN DECIDE!

ELEPHANT?

HEY THERE! IS THAT THE *ELEPHANT'S HEAD* AND A BALL OR IS IT A *QUESTION MARK?*

LOOK, LOOK, LOOK!

LOOK AT THE **WHITE DOTS** THAT
INTERSECT THE **GRAY LINES.**

A-MAZE-iNG!

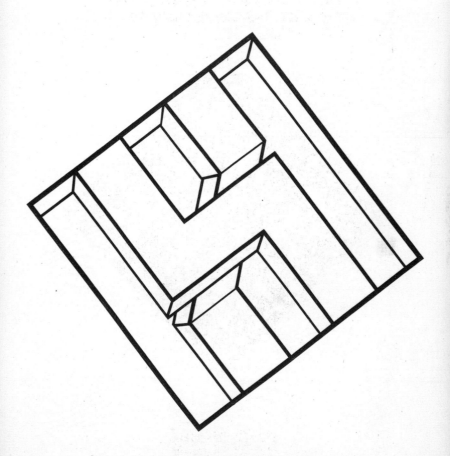

THINK YOU CAN FIND YOUR WAY **OUT** OF THIS **MIXED-UP MAZE?** IT'S AN **IMPOSSIBLE FIGURE!**

DO THE WAVE!

THIS PATTERN LOOKS LIKE IT'S **MOVING,** DOESN'T IT? IN FACT, IF YOU LOOK **LONG ENOUGH,** IT ALMOST LOOKS **3-D!**

MOOD SWINGS!

THIS LOOKS LIKE ONE **HAPPY COUPLE,** BUT
WHEN THINGS GET TURNED **UPSIDE DOWN,**
THEIR **MOODS** CHANGE DRASTICALLY!

IN THE BOX THINKING!

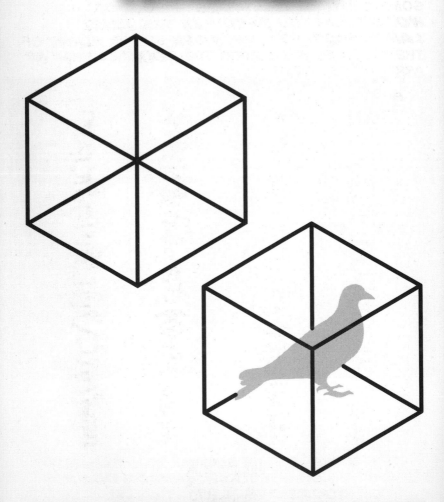

IS THIS A *SOLID DIAMOND* OR A *HOLLOW BIRD CAGE?* YOU *DECIDE!*

SAY WHAT?!

SOME **OPTICAL ILLUSIONS** ARE OUT OF THIS **WORLD!** CAN YOU **DECIPHER** THIS **ALIEN LANGUAGE?** FOLD THE **PAGE** SO THE **POINT** OF THE **"A"** ARROW TOUCHES THE **POINT** OF THE **"B"** ARROW, THEN **TRY!**

A ⟶   ⟵ B

GOOD-BYE!

PUZZLE

IS THIS ANOTHER *PUZZLE* OR IS THIS *THE END?*
TURN THE PAGE *UPSIDE DOWN* FOR THE *ANSWER!*